AND TO THE UNMARRIED I SAY

THINGS TO CONSIDER BEFORE SAYING, I DO

DARYL O'NEIL

And To the Unmarried I Say...
Things to Consider Before Saying I Do

Mailing address:
Ruach/Zion Covenant Church International
1380 Mitchell Road
Aurora, Illinois 60505

For speaking engagements please contact us at
Ruach Covenant Church International
Post Office Box 5619
River Forest, Illinois 60305
630-966-0200
 Daryl ONeil
 @defendcovenant
www.ruachinternational.com
email: ruachchurch@aol.com

Copyright ©2005
ISBN #978-1-943343-66-9

Cover design by: Crain Barnes
Cover illustration is protected by the 1976 United States Copyright Act.

ACKNOWLEDGEMENTS

I would like to offer special thanks and gratitude to those who have helped shape and mold the man and the message I share with you in this resource.

I thank my Lord and Savior Jesus Christ for His great love and His great work in my life through the Holy Spirit.

Blessings to my wife, Denice, and sons, Caleb and Judah, who are my helpers in growing in Christ-likeness. These are the precious jewels our Lord has chosen to help perfect in me His ways. May each of you know always, I love and am learning to love you more than you know or can believe!

Blessings to my mother Willie O'Neil. You have always sacrificed to permit me to have the best and to have the opportunity to achieve. You have been one of my biggest supporters. I pray I have made you proud. I love you.

Blessings to my aunt Annette Thomas. Even though you are present with the Lord, your prayers and words, "stay focused and do what you are called to do" help and continue to help fuel the ministry I steward on Christ's behalf. I will always be grateful. You were my second mom! I love and honor you.

Blessing to my dad, Ralph O'Neil Jr. Thank you for your love, prayers and continued support, although we have had our moments, I honor you and I love you.

Blessings to my Apostle and shepherd, John Eckhardt, who, with his wife, Pastor Wanda, and the Crusaders Church of Chicago family, have created great pathways in the spirit and the natural through years of teaching, impartation and encouragement for me to follow in growing from a son to a father in apostolic grace. Thanks for taking a chance to release me in ministry.

Blessings to Pastors Elton and Donna Watkins and Prophet Helen Mitchell, incredible friends who serve with me in leading two wonderful communities of faith for the glory of the Lord. I love you for your prayers, encouragement, diligence, faithfulness and friendship.

Blessings to Kevin Leal, my prophetic Barnabas, who taught me, "you are anointed to be you!" May God continue to bless you, Karen and all you steward on behalf of Christ.

Theophilus and Valarie Jones for loving me and believing in the message enough to host and support the first "And to the Unmarried I say Conferences." I love you and may the Lord continue to richly bless your ministry.

Blessings to all the faith family of Ruach Covenant Church International and Zion Covenant Church International for your love, prayers and support of the ministry of Christ within me. I am grateful to God to co-labor with you all in advancing the kingdom of God in the earth. Thanks to the churches 'doin the work'! We are local communities with global impact.

And To The Unmarried I Say...

TABLE OF CONTENTS

INTRODUCTION

Several years ago I preached a message in our faith community (church) that was inspired by the Holy Spirit, to help with one of the major decisions an unmarried person will have to face in his or her life. The title of the message was simply, B4U Say "I Do."

The response to this teaching surprised and startled me. Many individuals came to me after service and stated, "I wish I had had the opportunity to get this insight or provocation of thought before I got married."

I thought or assumed a person, before making such a decision, would surely have to get some advice or instruction. I thought they would counsel with people either successful in their marriages or at least someone who was knowledgeable about relationships and spiritually mature. I did not know how wrong I was.

One of my desires as a shepherd is to prepare individuals to succeed in any endeavor in life. Christianity is based on principles of the King and His Kingdom. These principles **when applied** can produce success in any life. Marriage is a sacrament and vocation, I have witnessed people crash and burn attempting to be married. I have seen, first hand, the wreckage of an unfruitful marriage.

In society today, the divorce rate is alarmingly over fifty- percent. I am also sad to say, among people who profess to have a relationship with the Lord, the divorce rate is equal to or higher than those who do not confess a strong faith in God. That is one out of every two marriages.

I am a man on a mission! In order to protect and bless the purpose of God for your life and those you love, I write this book to attempt to help stop this trend at the root.

Before you say I Do.

Something has to be done to change this trend of non-fruitfulness. I believe there is an answer. I write this resource with this in mind. I believe there is no such thing as a perfect marriage or the perfect person. If certain principles of the kingdom of God are applied, a person can know if they will be able to have a great deal of success being married or should not marry at all.

While I believe you can determine who will be the best choice for you to spend your life with, I want to suggest a new thought for some. I do not declare it to be the only view, but another view.

There is a widely held view that there is only one person in the whole world for you. I don't think this is quite the truth.

Thinking like this will limit the possibilities for a person to find a mate or be found, if they are looking to be married. I do not believe you should have limited possibilities.

May I suggest, if any two people practice the principles of scripture towards each other, each define love based on God's definition of love, are friends sharing common interests and will work together in reaching their goals, they can have a happy life together. It is important we make proper evaluations.

In this resource, I also want to create dialog concerning the gift of being unmarried. I want to suggest to you the idea that God on purpose, creates people who have no desire to be married and help them be celebrated and find their true calling in this life.

In undertaking the assignment of creating dialog supporting the gift of being unmarried, I run the risk of being judged as one who is against marriage. That would not be an accurate judgment. This is not a resource to discourage marriage. I desire for people to enjoy true covenantal love. But, I also feel a mandate, as an apostolic father, to bless those who may have the gift of being unmarried and create faith for their gift in the Body of Christ.

This resource is **not** all inclusive of *everything* you can consider before saying 'I Do'. **I desire to provoke thought about things you may not have considered as you seek the Creator for the wisdom you need to make such an important decision.**

Do I get married or do I choose to remain unmarried?

Please ask the one who gave you life! It is my endeavor to give you a tool, whereby you can make sound practical decisions.

There are those who are married who may find things to reflect on. Perhaps you may find some things to apply to strengthen your own marriage. You may know someone who is unmarried who will benefit by passing this resource on as a gift.

And to the unmarried I say...before saying 'I Do' consider these things. Let us explore them together and may you be happy ever after!

CHAPTER ONE

WISDOM IS THE PRINCIPAL THING

A wise *man* will hear and increase learning, And a man of understanding will attain wise counsel, **Proverbs 1:5**

Get Wisdom!

I want to begin this work with some faith-filled declarations. You are an unmarried person who is wise, or you may be married and seeking wisdom for someone who is unmarried.

You may be widowed and contemplating getting married again. Or, you are divorced and may want to remarry and do it wisely. You already know the value of getting knowledge. Learning is important to you. You are a person of understanding and know it is best to have wise counsel around.

For by wise counsel you will wage your own war, And in a multitude of counselors, *there is* safety. **Proverbs 24:6**

One of God's great blessings to us is the gift of

wisdom and wise counsel. Before you say I do, never get married without counseling. There are many people making life altering decisions without seeking someone else's insight. This is sad but true. We need to pursue counsel because we may lie to ourselves. Consider this:

Counsel (or Consultation) is the act of exchanging opinions and ideas. It is advice or guidance solicited from a person who is knowledgeable in the arena from which you are attempting to make a good decision.

The dictionary also defines counsel as a wise plan of action.

Before you say I do, it is important for you to have a plan of action from courting to the big wedding day. Counsel (a plan of action) can provide safety. I believe it is the will of God for you to be safe. Counsel is best when used to help **make a correct decision,** not after the decision is made.

Marriage represents something so powerful in the spirit it will create and open a door for warfare. When we speak of marriage, we are not just talking about two people getting together for the sake of being able to have spiritually legalized sexual relations. We are speaking of a sacrament representing Christ and His church. We are talking about something which expresses the kingdom of God.

With wise counsel, you will be able to wage war in the spirit, defeat every strategy designed to cause decisions to be made selfishly...and win!

A wise plan for courting, character examination, future life's goals and dreams will provide safety for all parties involved.

A wise minister of the gospel, Apostle Louis Greenup, once said to me, "Show me your friends and I will predict your future." He also prayed this quite humorous prayer, "God deliver me from stupid people!" To that prayer I say, Amen!

There are two verses of scripture which speak to the need of a person to have insight from outside of ourselves.

> All the ways of a man are clean in his own eyes; but the LORD weighs the spirits. **Proverbs 16:2**

> Every way of a man is right in his own eyes: but the LORD ponders the hearts. **Proverbs 21:2**

These two verses are clear reminders we will not always tell ourselves the truth. So when it comes to deciding to get married, we need counsel to help get a plan of action.

When we have to make big decisions, tough decisions, or need wise direction, the last thing we need are people with no wisdom. There are individuals who have made major decisions in their life without getting any counsel. Some people experienced no problems. However, many, many more will tell you from experience, they wished they had gotten counsel (a plan of action) from a wise person or people **before** making such a decision. As I endeavor to provoke your thinking, I want to challenge you before you say I do, get counseling.

Get wisdom!

I want to declare to you there is wisdom available from God. He releases it through people here on earth to speak and guide us on His behalf to bring blessing into our lives. Get wisdom!

> For the LORD gives wisdom; From His mouth *come* knowledge and understanding; **Proverbs 2:6**

It is important to understand if a marriage is going to be successful, wisdom must be a building tool.

In defining wisdom the dictionary says <u>"Wisdom is the ability to discern or judge what is true or right; insight.</u>" If we look at this in relationship to our Creator, He is the Great Judge, He is Truth and He is Right. He is our insight. How does He speak? Through the principle of His words!

It says in scripture, "Wisdom has built her house and has hewn out her seven pillars..." Wisdom does the work necessary for establishing a solid foundation. The number seven in Holy Scripture speaks of divine perfection, maturity and completeness. When she (wisdom) does her work, it is a complete work. Wisdom will protect you. If you are male wisdom will protect you from the "strange woman" who flatters with her lips. If you are female wisdom will protect you from the evil man who has "perverse speech"

Proverbs speaks of how wisdom prepares a strong, fortified and abundant place for those to come and receive all the instruction they need to be successful in any endeavor. Then wisdom invites us to come and partake of what she has to offer:

> "Whoever *is* simple, let him turn in here!" *As for* him who lacks understanding, she says to him, "Come, eat of my bread and drink of the wine I have mixed. Forsake foolishness and live, and go in the way of understanding. **Proverbs 9:4-6**

The bible speaks concerning not being ignorant of satan's devices.

Ignorance is what must be overcome. Also, it speaks of the wiles of the devil. If I can simplify these words, devices or wiles, each speak of strategy and plans. If you are going to have a successful life married or unmarried, you need a plan.

One plan of the enemy of our lives is to provoke us to foolishness! Listen to what the word of God states :

> The fool has said in his heart, "*There is* no God." They are corrupt, they have done abominable works, there is none who does good. The LORD looks down from heaven upon the children of men, to see if there are any who understand, who seek God. **Psalm 14:1-2**

Verse 2 is a key to the plan of satan. Keeping us as children of God from praying and inquiring of God, making us a fool. When we pray we get wisdom, a plan of action, from the Lord's mouth.

For the LORD gives wisdom; From His mouth *come* knowledge and understanding; **Proverbs 2:6**

Wisdom entails having a plan. God's plan will always defeat satan's plan when applied. A fool will not get help, even when lacking understanding.

Now, there is another interesting word, understanding. Let's define it.

<u>Understanding, according to Webster's dictionary, means to perceive; to comprehend the significance of something.</u>

We must flee foolishness, know the significance of the decision being contemplated and make a strong plan! You then will be blessed.

May I make a suggestion? Before you say I do, get counsel to determine **if** you should get married.

As an overseer of several ministries, I cannot even count the number of times I have had people come to me saying they wanted to receive counsel because they were getting married.

Often times they had already bought rings, set a date, began joining bank accounts and put money down on a house. I would think to myself, "what possibly could this couple want from me other than for me to agree with what has already been planned." May I suggest strongly, **Please do not leave your pastor or overseer in this position.**

I want to share this thought on behalf of many pastors, who have thought or experienced this feeling and would like to get this message out: PLEASE GIVE US A CHANCE TO HELP YOU! DON'T PUT US IN A POSITION TO FEEL LIKE VILLAINS OR BAD PEOPLE, IF THE ONE YOU INTEND TO MARRY IS NOT THE ONE OR THE TIMING IS NOT RIGHT BASED ON COUNSEL AFTER ALL YOUR PLANS HAVE BEEN MADE!

I want to share a couple of stories, that are unfortunately true, of couples who made plans first without counsel. Please don't let the moral of the stories be lost! I tell these stories not to inspire fear in you, the reader. My desire is to provoke sober thinking about a very important sacrament, marriage. Counsel is very important.

A couple called to receive counsel because they were getting married. They had already set a date, reserved the place for the reception, exchanged engagement rings and mailed out all the invitations. I thought, "God how can I help them? They have already made their decision."

We started the counseling sessions and, after three sessions, I determined this was certainly not the timing of God for this couple to get married (if they should have gotten married at all). I felt compelled to tell them, "Even though you have done all these things, for your happiness it is best you postpone the wedding!"

Well you can imagine their response. You can probably envision this couple wrestling with thoughts like, "What are people going to think? What about all the money we spent? I do not want the embarrassment!" There were, I am sure, a host of other thoughts too.

After the first few months, when the wedding was over, reality set in. The challenges I foresaw began to surface early in the marriage and there was lamenting of their having made the decision. It did not have to be that way. The couple is still married today, yet difficulty has been their portion more than the joy and blessing of a happy covenant.

Marriage should be a celebration, not toleration. When there is celebration there is joy, happiness, sacrifice, harmony and forward movement. When there is toleration, usually there is mistrust, disappointment, frustration, anger and stagnation. If you are desiring to get married, choose a partner who will celebrate you. Do not choose a partner who tolerates or puts up with you.

The second story still brings great sadness when I think of the tragic results to a beautiful daughter in the Lord. After counseling this couple, in my heart I could not violate what was evident to my natural eyes and my spirit. The young man presenting himself to marry Jane (not her real name) had all the right words, but not the right tangible attitude or fruit.

Jane's reasons for getting married were influenced by others desires, including wanting to have children before her grandmother passed away. Jane was convinced it was of the Lord. I was not.

I chose not to perform the wedding ceremony and so did another pastor, who was a friend of Jane's. Another minister did perform the ceremony and from all reports, it was a beautiful wedding. Unfortunately, a wedding is not a marriage.

This couple was married and after just about eight days, she was dead! Her new husband did not physically harm her. However, stories surfacing after her death indicated, he was not the man he portrayed himself to be. It caused a great deal of stress. It aggravated an old heart condition she had lived with since birth.

I often wonder if Jane had learned what I perceived and communicated to them in counsel but they felt too far-gone into their plans to stop them.

Talking with one of her close friends weeks after, I learned she had realized she made a mistake. There are other stories I could share but I think you get the point. May I say, if there are any concerns right up to days before the wedding, before you say I do, get wise counsel.

I remember standing before our congregation and suggesting to all the unmarried women who wanted to experience the hoopla surrounding a wedding, "Let's get it on!" Let us let you dress up, invite all your friends, plan a big party and go on vacation afterwards. Let us get the idea of a wedding out of your system, because a wedding is not a marriage!

For every vocation, in the world, where people can adversely affect the lives of others, doctors, dentists, airline pilots, school bus drivers etc., there is a great deal of training before permitting you to work professionally with other lives involved.

Marriage and parenting are two vocations where many start and get on the job training. This sometimes makes the job very, very difficult. Counseling before hand is training and preparation for success in dealing with this very important calling, **if** it is your calling.

Get wisdom!

- *Chapter Two* -

UNMARRIED: TO BE OR NOT TO BE?

> Or do you not know that your body is the temple of the Holy Spirit *who is* in you, whom you have from God, and **you are not your own?** For you were bought at a price; therefore glorify God in your body and in your spirit, which are God's. **1 Corinthians 6:19-20**

Before you say I do, I think it is important to examine this question.

Am I designed by God to be unmarried or married?

As I began this book, the original title of this chapter was, "Single: To Be or Not To Be." I had to submit to a new understanding. The bible very rarely refers to unmarried people as single.

They were referred to either as a virgins or unmarried or widows. For some this will be a revelation, as it was for me.

We will need to define the concept of being single, but the issue is whether to be unmarried or married.

I want to share a statement which seems to govern life, "Our definition determines our destination." What we believe words to mean shape our conclusions or judgments. It is important to know as an unmarried person what it means to be single.

I will move in and out of this chapter identifying what it means to be single. Those who choose to be unmarried will have to be single, *by definition*. The truth is those who are married must be single. You will see what I mean in a the next chapter!

We have a life to live on earth. It is not ours. It belongs to our Creator. There is fantasy and there is reality. The reality for us all is we have nothing to do with how we get here. We have nothing to do with whose family we are born into or what race we are born.

I can think of a few last names that would have sounded great after my first name. For instance, Trump, Rockefeller, Gates, Johnson or Winfrey. How about you? OK, O'Neil sounds great too! I would like to have chosen where I was born. New Zealand, Hawaii, Australia, Jamaica, Arizona, just to name a few. I think you get my point.

If we have nothing to do with our being here, perhaps we are supposed to live our life for someone else. Maybe the one who gave us life, our Creator? I believe, it is important to consider this question, am I to live unmarried or be married?

We live in a society which puts pressure on unmarried people to make them feel as if they are not married or married by a certain age something is wrong with them.

I want to state very emphatically, *there is nothing wrong with being unmarried. It can be a gift from God.*

There are many insensitive people always asking and badgering their relatives, friends or acquaintances with questions such as, when are you getting married? Are you dating anyone yet? You know you're getting older? It makes you feel like saying, "mind your business!"

Many times a young man who chooses not to get married is considered gay. Women, who have not gotten married by a certain age are thought to be "old maids." This of course is not kind, fair, or right. In fact, a believer, being unmarried provides a great opportunity to totally focus on serving the Lord without distraction. Listen to words from scripture through the mouth of the Apostle Paul:

> But I want you to be without care. He who is unmarried cares for the things of the Lord—how he may please the Lord. But he who is married cares about the things of the world—how he may please *his* wife. **1 Corinthians 7:32-33**

I want to give a word of encouragement to every unmarried person, who has insensitive influencers (people) in their lives not to be provoked to make a decision based upon being shamed or having reproach heaped upon you.

Do not make a covenant with another person based upon others thoughts of who you are. You are fearfully and wonderfully made of the Lord. In Christ, you are accepted not rejected. I encourage you to break free of the witchcraft of others.

When I use the term witchcraft, the holy scriptures in the book of Galatians 5 lists it as a work of the flesh.

Simply put, witchcraft is a selfish desire of another person to get you to do what they believe you should by using the power of intimidation, manipulation and domination. God does not lead anyone by fear. God is love.

Let us now define the word single and then look at some scriptures, which offer some interesting thoughts to those who are unmarried.

The Webster's dictionary defines being single as **being separate, unique and whole.**

- **Separate**: to become distinct; individual, complete

- **Unique**: one and only; extraordinary; rare

- **Whole**: in sound health; not diseased or injured; healed; not broken, damaged or defective; total; a complete unit physically, mentally, socially and spiritually.

We must also define the word alone because unmarried people often get attacked with loneliness and attempt to get rid of the feeling by getting married or through dating instead of becoming single, by definition.

- **Alone**: separated from others; not including

anyone or anything else; detached; isolated; removed; solitary.

God, in the Bible stated, "It is not good for man to be alone." God then gave Adam a helper comparable to himself. Eve was separate, unique and capable of accomplishing what she was designed for.

Before two people get married, I believe it is important each person be truly single by definition. May I say it again? Separate, unique, and whole!

If you or the person you are contemplating making a life's commitment to are not whole, the time to marry is not now. **I did not say never, but NOT NOW.**

Each of you must be able to be healthy enough on your own to do the thing YOU were created to do. Once you come together, there should be two whole people, not two isolated, hurt or detached from life people.

I'd like to share an illustration given me by one of the elders in our local church, Dominick Foster. I hope this will help make this concept a bit clearer.

Think for a moment of a key ring with seven keys that will open seven different doors. Each key is single (unique, separate and whole). All the keys are joined by a common ring. Each key has worth and is complete and can do the job for which it is designed, but they are not alone. I want to affirm your wholeness. Be whole!

Paul: Unmarried but not alone

If you are unmarried and have strong faith in God, you should consider these words of a powerful unmarried man who was single by definition. Paul, the apostle wrote:

> Now concerning the things of which you wrote to me: *It is* good for a man not to touch a woman. **1 Corinthians 7:1**

For I wish that all men were even as I myself. But each one has his own gift from God, one in this manner and another in that.

> But I say to the unmarried and to the widows: It is good for them if they remain even as I am; but if they cannot exercise self-control, let them marry. For it is better to marry than to burn *with passion. (emphasis added by author)*. **1 Corinthians 7:7-9**

Here the Apostle Paul is answering questions concerning marriage and makes a very compelling case for staying unmarried.

First of all he calls being unmarried, the grace of self-control, a gift from God. *There is no written law that states you have to get married, if you are unmarried.* Being unmarried is just as much a gift as being married is a gift. To the believer who is unmarried the word of God says:

But I want you to be without care. He who is unmarried cares for the things of the Lord—how he may please the Lord. But he who is married cares about the things of the world—how he may please *his* wife. There is a difference between a wife and a virgin.

The unmarried woman cares about the things of the Lord, that she may be holy both in body and in spirit. But, she who is married cares about the things of the world—how she may please *her* husband. And this I say for your own profit, not that I may put a leash on you, but for what is proper, and that you may serve the Lord without distraction. **1 Corinthians 7:32-35**

According to Paul, the *ultimate* for an unmarried person is **not** to be distracted from whole-heartedly serving God. Sometimes life is so filled with cares it is possible to forget the word of God saying we were created for His good pleasure.

I want to remind you some of the greatest people discussed in the bible were unmarried. THERE IS NOTHING WRONG WITH BEING UNMARRIED. In order to reverse the trend in our culture to look at the unmarried as lepers, I must continue to state this truth. Christ was unmarried. There was no shame on Him for this. There should be none on you, if you make a decision to stay unmarried.

Before you say I do, make sure you don't have the gift of being unmarried. If you know you do not have the gift of self-control, then it is better to get married instead of burning with ungratified desire (lust). I think it is of the utmost importance for every unmarried person to inquire of the Lord in prayer whether it is **His** will for you to be married.

Holy Scriptures speak of the fact those who confess a hope in Christ are not their own anymore. If we belong to Him, truly we owe it to Him to ask what is His desire for our lives.

As an observation, one of the reasons I perceive there are so many divorces in society is because there are not many voices creating enough of a dialogue to stir faith for the gift of being unmarried.

While making this statement, I am not advocating against marriage. I just think it is important to create faith for all gifts of God. The dialog I want to create is to raise a level of thinking about what Jesus teaches of some who are born into the world with this gift.

To further clarify my point, when there are teachings in the church on the subject of healing, those who have a passion or gifting in this area will discover who they are!

If a person is gifted in prophecy or one of the dimensions of the prophetic, when prophets teach on the subject, revelation is released and people are able to discover or get faith to trust God with their lives in this area. So it is with those who are born with the gift to be unmarried. The word of God say "so then faith comes by hearing and hearing by the word of God." (Romans 10:17) The ability to trust or have confidence in God is based on hearing the word of God.

I believe in the days to come there will be more

teaching in the church concerning being unmarried and single by definition (unique, complete and whole) and it will cause faith to come alive to live unmarried, but not alone.

- **Unmarried another view**

Let's look at another passage of scripture. I have attended worship services regularly since I confessed a hope in Christ at the age of 15 (currently I am 54 years of age) and have never heard anyone teach on the subject of eunuchs on a Sunday or mid week service although it is clearly in the bible:

His disciples said to Him, "If such is the case of the man with *his* wife, it is better not to marry."

> But He said to them, "All cannot accept this saying, but only *those* to whom it has been given: For there are eunuchs who were born thus from *their* mother's womb, and there are eunuchs who were made eunuchs by men, and there are eunuchs who have made themselves eunuchs for the kingdom of heaven's sake. He who is able to accept *it,* let him accept *it."*
> **Matthew 19:10-12**

While Jesus is discussing the subject of marriage and divorce with His followers, He states something that never seems to be discussed much in the church. He talks about *eunuchs* for the kingdoms sake.

A eunuch is defined as a male deprived of the testes or external genitals. Eunuchs were regarded as especially **trustworthy** in the Ancient Near East and thus were **frequently employed in royal service**. The Greek term translated eunuch is literally **one in charge** of a bed, a reference to the practice of using eunuchs as keepers of harems (Esther: 2:3, 6, 15). A "eunuch for the sake of the kingdom of heaven" (Matt. 19:12) is likely a metaphor for one choosing unmarried life in order to be more useful in kingdom work.

This passage intrigues me, because we are not talking simply about another human being making this statement.

We are speaking about Jesus Christ, the Son of God. If there is anyone who knows whether someone is born into the earth with the gift to be unmarried, it is the Creator.

He states there are three types of eunuchs, those born from their mothers wombs, those who are made eunuchs of men and those who have made themselves eunuch for the kingdom of heaven's sake.

Who is creating faith for this gift? Who is going to create faith for this gift?

As an apostolic father, I think it is important to create faith for this gift. The apostle Paul thought so. If you are unmarried, perhaps you were born with this gift. It is not negative. It is powerful.

I know the word eunuch does not seem to inspire anything positive, yet a study of the function and character traits of such individuals in the bible reveal a potent, fruitful and governmental person.

In the light of these statements, I want to suggest there is a place in Christ, where true covenant mentality and actions are developed.

It is called "eunuch for the kingdom's sake."

Eunuchs, when looked at beyond the obvious understanding of being emasculated men, set forth powerful virtues and characteristics which I believe can be pursued, developed and provide protection to any unmarried person whether you want to be married or not.

Jesus' use of the metaphor eunuchs for the kingdom's sake is a powerful look at a place an unmarried person can function in, while being prepared for their king (Christ).

Here are some things I think you should know which are revealed in scripture to help change your former thoughts about eunuchs:

- Eunuchs have a prophetic blessing over their life

- Eunuchs operated in a priestly function

- Eunuchs were some of the most faithful, loyal, dedicated, and trustworthy individuals ever.

- Eunuchs served among royalty. They understood the kings needs. The king's likes and dislikes. What kinds of food the king ate. What the king liked to look at. The eunuchs were to really have the heart of the king. They were thought of very highly.

- Many eunuchs were governmental and had oversight over others.

- Eunuchs were fiercely focused (not distracted) functioning in one of the most power places in the kingdom, as a steward.

- Eunuchs also were often times responsible for the preparation of those who would go before the king.

It is a powerful place or position to live from. Think about that!

Question. What happens to the young man or young woman who does not have any desire for sexual relations with members of the opposite sex?

In our society, there is so much pressure to get married and have a family. If no one teaches on the subject matter of eunuchs, two negative lifestyle consequences begin to fight for this life which from the womb was meant for the Kingdom of God to advance His purposes.

One such negative lifestyle is divorce. I want to pose a question. Could one reason for the high divorce rate be many who were born to be unmarried ended up getting married?

Maybe a person, who had the gift of being unmarried, got married just for the sake of someone else so they would not look like they were abnormal. There are many different reasons why people break their covenant of marriage, but I believe one of the least discussed is they were not born to be married!

I will make this statement perhaps a few more times, but Before you say I do, seek your Creator to find out if you are to remain unmarried. **Being unmarried is not being alone!**

I believe another negative impact of not discussing the positive aspect of being unmarried and encouraging those who are, is that many have ended up choosing to have alternative lifestyle sexual relationships. Because there is no real dialogue about the subject of eunuchs, there are many who are born with no desire for the opposite sex or are 'confused' about their sexuality. This sometimes opens the door for the 'spirit of homosexuality'.

I personally believe a lot of the confusion experienced by some males and females when it comes to homosexual feelings, has to do with the fact no one really discusses the truth concerning eunuchs. Jesus makes very clear people can be born as eunuchs, from their mothers womb.

We hear discussion of people being born gay or lesbian. I think sexual orientation is learned behavior. I believe if God gives a life, He gives it with a purpose. The discussion of eunuchs has to be examined. The one who created all things knows what our purpose is.

If you, as one who is unmarried, grow up without ever being told it is possible from your mother's womb to not desire the opposite sex **because you were separated for the Lord's purpose**, you might be cheated of a fulfilled life as one who is unmarried.

As an observation, I think one of the great needs of unmarried people in churches all across America and the world is for ministry gifts to create faith in the heart of those who are called of God to be unmarried and single for Him!

The word of God is clear, faith comes by hearing and hearing by the word of God!

You can have such a positive effect on all humanity by pursuing which kingdom of the world (government, entertainment, finance, education etc.) God would desire you as an unmarried person to impact for Him. I feel here to emphasize, I believe in marriage, but there is no harm to desire to be unmarried.

The commitment to marry someone is making a statement most people have not even been able to test before making such a commitment. **Forsaking all others, I choose you.** I am hopeful there will be many willing to encourage those who are unmarried to sincerely ask God whether marriage is what His purpose is for them.

I have heard it said by the marriage doctor, Apostle Louis Greenup, "Love is blind, but marriage will open up both your eyes!"

In summary, we are all given life by God with a divine purpose. While unmarried, it is important to inquire of the Creator if it is His will for you to be married.

There is a gift of self control. Many people through shame, fear and embarrassment are making decisions to get married for the wrong reasons. Many are ending up divorced. Others are choosing alternate lifestyles.

Unmarried to be or not be? This is one important question because the covenant called marriage is serious.

- Chapter Three-

MARRIAGE IS SERIOUS

Now, it came to pass, when Jesus had finished these sayings, *that* He departed from Galilee and came to the region of Judea beyond the Jordan. And great multitudes followed Him, and He healed them there. The Pharisees also came to Him, testing Him, and saying to Him, "Is it lawful for a man to divorce his wife for *just* any reason?"

And He answered and said to them, "Have you not read that He who made *them* at the beginning *'made them male and female,'* and said, *'For this reason a man shall leave his father and mother and be joined to his wife, and the two shall become one flesh'*? So then, they are no longer two but one flesh. Therefore what God has joined together, let not man separate.

They said to Him, "Why then did Moses command to give a certificate of divorce, and to put her away?"

He said to them, "Moses, because of the hardness of your hearts, permitted you to divorce your wives, but from the beginning it was not so. And I say to you, whoever divorces his wife, except for sexual immorality, and marries another, commits adultery; and whoever marries her who is divorced commits adultery."

His disciples said to Him, "**If such is the case of the man with his wife, it is better not to marry." Matthew 19:3-10**

When I was a young man, I attended weddings where I would hear the preacher say, "marriage is nothing that should be entered into lightly." I second that motion. And third it too!

Marriage is serious. When Jesus was being tested by the Pharisees with a question about putting away (divorcing) your wife, Jesus gave a response which was sobering. He spoke of the level of commitment necessary and expected of two people entering into a marriage. The disciples in just overhearing Him talk to someone else about covenant and marriage said, **"It is better not to marry!"**

Jesus made it quite clear, God our Father considers the covenant of marriage binding. God is faithful. I believe He values faithfulness. Because God is faithful, I believe it is going to be very important to seek to marry someone who has this character trait of the Creator. God is love and the attribute of faithfulness is a characteristic of a loving person.

I looked up the word *faithful* and saw several synonyms that must be considered before saying I do. Loyal, devoted, trustworthy, dedicated, committed, dependable and believable.

Is the person I am contemplating sharing the rest of my life with demonstrating these attributes? Are they actively pursuing developing these attributes? Do I demonstrate these attributes? Am I pursuing developing these attributes?

In any type of lasting relationship, there must be faithfulness. If the person you are courting does not value these attributes and does not seek to demonstrate them, chances are they will be unfaithful. Faithfulness to a relationship has to be considered a spiritual thing. Faithfulness is a dimension of love. Faithfulness is visibly seen through selflessness.

Before you say I do, you must love yourself enough to find out if someone has the ability to be faithful. You must evaluate yourself honestly, if you are to be considered faithful. If you are an unmarried man or woman, you owe it to yourself to know what these words mean before you get involved in courting (dating) seriously.

Loyalty, devotion, trustworthiness, dedication, commitment, dependability, truthfulness, exactness and believability are all types of behavior visible to the eyes. These are also all very practical things you must see when a person is interacting with others. These attributes cannot be hidden. If they are there, they will come to the surface!

In the passage of scripture in Matthew 19, Jesus states that except for sexual immorality a person divorcing his/her spouse would be committing adultery, if they join in union with another person. Let's define adultery:

ADULTERY: is the act of unfaithfulness in marriage that occurs when one of the marriage partners voluntarily engages in sexual intercourse with a person other than the marriage partner.

The gospel is the good news of the Kingdom of God. The Kingdom has a King and His name is Jesus. The Kingdom also has principles. When it comes to marriage, heaven dictates what we can and cannot do in the covenant called marriage.

Covenant is a word every unmarried person should have written in their heart, especially believers. One definition for the word covenant is: the agreement of two parties to be **committed** to their relationship.

The word committed is a synonym of the word faithful. If I don't understand marriage is a covenant and covenant needs commitment, how can I fulfill purpose in this area? The kingdom functions by covenant and faithfulness.

Before you say I do, examine and consider in a practical way the natural expression of faithfulness. Take time to recite synonyms for the word faithful and watch how you begin to view life! You do not want to marry a person who has tendencies of adultery. These are attributes opposite to faithfulness.

A study of the doctrine concerning adultery should be enough for many people to very carefully examine whether they have the ability or the desire to commit for life to a relationship with another individual.

Just a thought to consider, how many unmarried people have entered into adulterous marriages according to what Jesus has taught?

Courting vs. Dating: Discovering Faithfulness

There is spiritual warfare going on in the lives of those who have chosen to walk in the ways of Christ. Each unmarried believer *must know* they are being shaped into the image (exact likeness) of Christ. One of the most important aspects of a kingdom believer is we are being developed into people of covenant. God is a covenant keeper. Everything God does is in the context of covenant.

With this in mind, I must remind you there is war going on in the spirit realm between covenant keepers and fornicators. Make no mistake about it. When you as an unmarried person repent of your sins and surrender your heart and life, you become joined and bound to Him in covenant.

It is saying, based on the definition of covenant, I am agreeing to be committed to our relationship. It is a covenant, a promise of trust based upon your word.

The reason it is important to view our relationship as believers this way is to create space for understanding how fornication, as a principle, can be taught before ever being engaged in as an act.

And unto the angel of the church in Thyatira write; These things saith the Son of God, who hath his eyes like unto a flame of fire, and his feet are like fine brass; I know thy works, and charity, and service, and faith, and thy patience, and thy works; and the last to be more than the first.

> Notwithstanding I have a few things against thee, because thou suffer that woman Jezebel, which calls herself a prophetess, to teach and to seduce my servants to commit fornication, and to eat things sacrificed unto idols. And I gave her space to repent of her fornication; and she repented not. Behold, I will cast her into a bed, and them that commit adultery with her into great tribulation, except they repent of their deeds. And I will kill her children with death; and all the churches shall know that I am he which search the reins and hearts: and I will give unto every one of you according to your works. **Revelations 2:18-23**

In the old testament, often times when the Lord wanted to help the nation of Israel to understand their spiritual condition in relationship to the Lord, He would use terms like idolatry, whoredoms and whoring.

These are all terms to express the idea of unfaithfulness to the promise to be committed to their agreement. It is with this in mind that I submit the words of Christ concerning the church at Thyatira.

There was a person of influence in the church named Jezebel, whose name means un-covenanted or un-husbanded one. This speaks of no covenant. I believe, while we can look at this passage and conclude she was teaching people to commit acts of sexual immorality and idolatry, we might be remiss not to look at the spiritual dimension of this action. She was teaching God's servants not to be committed to their agreement or promise with Him and His words and leading them into having a relationship with Him with no commitment. This has never been acceptable to God and never will be.

There are many teachings in the church on the spirit of Jezebel.

I want to share another view of the work of this spirit. It is a spirit every unmarried covenant person will have to deal with. I want to submit a new way of looking at what the spirit of Jezebel really causes when it is in operation in the life of a man or woman. It teaches people to not be committed to covenant relationships. Jezebel seduces and teaches the doctrine of fornication. It is a covenant breaking spirit.

I have often advocated for unmarried people not to go out alone (dating) with an individual you are interested in getting to know more about. Usually, too much time alone with someone you have begun dating will lead to fornication. I say this because intimacy is bred by talking first. I have always encouraged (courting) group activities to help develop covenant friendship first.

Let me make it very clear there is a difference between courting and dating. Dating can lead to fornication. Courting helps develop covenant skills. The word fornication comes from the Greek word porneia, which means all forms of sexual impurity. This is its natural expression in the earth.

I want to identify spiritual fornication as being involved in relationships in which there is no real commitment. It is a selfish relationship. Remember, God is love. Love is not selfish. I believe dating is where selfishness is learned at an early age and then over a period of time perfected. Just a thought.

I would like to provoke you to examine a bit more closely what is communicated when people date versus court.

Consider this, in our society, it is nothing to begin having boyfriends and girlfriends at an early age. Many times children as young as 12 years old begin 'going steady'.

While this may seem innocent, the seeds for trouble later in life are being sown. They will not be seeds which will only affect relationships but will also affect prosperity.

In dating, it is usually I am in the relationship as long as it is good for me. If it gets tough, I get out and get a new relationship. In dating, it is easy to learn how to have multiple boyfriends and girlfriends. I want to submit dating is where covenant breaking is taught. The principle of if the relationship is not working for me, find another one which works. Many times this way of thinking leads to unfaithfulness (cheating).

We must flee fornication. This way of thinking will

produce poverty. God never blesses outside of covenant. Don't be deceived.

Courting. Now there's an ancient word. It is defined as discovering common interests and developing covenant friendships by engaging in conversation and activities with common interests while around others (friends, family, church, family etc.).

Courting is when two people learn about each other and work towards a possible committed relationship. It is also a time for observing faithfulness.

Courting is a time when, while around others, you can watch and see how each other deal with different people and personality types. How a person treats others in different environments can be an indicator of how they will treat you.

Learning likes and dislikes takes time. It takes time to discover if we have healthy communication skills. It takes time to discover if a person is really selfish rather than selfless. When I was a teenager there was a song by a group called DeBarge that was rather prophetic entitled, "Time will Reveal." Learn the art of patience and let time reveal who you are with. Do not get in a hurry. Watch.

If a person consistently demonstrates the attributes described by the afore mentioned synonyms for faithfulness while courting you, you have a person with whom you can possibly build a life with. A personal examination of our own selves in these areas will help us be a good mate for someone else too. Ponder that!

Something to consider: while courting there should be people with each of your personalities in the mix to see how a potential mate will deal with your personality type when the person is not you. Adversity during this time will reveal the real person. I want to suggest we are not the person we really are when things are going well. The real 'us' comes out when there is difficulty.

Do not take those times lightly in the person courting you and in yourself.

Before you say I Do, while courting please know, adversity is a key to identifying a true friend. A friend is who you want to spend the rest of your life with. The bible has a lot to say on the subject of friendship. True friends are born in times of adversity.

Consider this:

> A friend loves at all times, and a brother is born for adversity. **Proverbs 17:17**

> Faithful are the wounds of a friend; but the kisses of an enemy are deceitful. **Proverbs 27:6**

> Greater love hath no man than this, that a man lay down his life for his friends. **John 15:13**

These three verses of scripture are packed with the essence of what is produced during courting. There is a dimension of relationship called "greater love" which can never be obtained without friendship. Before you say I do, you want to know the person you are going to spend the rest of your life with is going to be willing to lay their life down for you. The principle in this is connected with friendship.

Another important trait to be discovered during courting is honesty. A friend loves you enough to not deceive you. Long lasting covenant is based on trust and truth. These are qualities of a real friend.

Don't marry a lover. Marry a friend! Courting is different than dating.

Dating in our society has seemingly been reduced to trying to get someone who will be a first night sex partner or some external show piece to impress others. That is why I continue to encourage and stress courting. Often when we were going out back in the day, we got ready to "hook up" with someone. The goal was not a commitment but to do the "wild thing"(oops! I meant have sexual relations).

Usually in dating there is a great deal of deception. We put on our best clothes, smells, looks and attitudes. After a while, we start to become ourselves. We start out opening the doors for the ladies, but after awhile they open the door for themselves. We start by bringing flowers and being romantic and end up with no romance at all.

Because dating is usually about some selfish interest, there is a great deal of hurt and disappointment. "I want people to think I have the cutest boyfriend or I want to have as many beautiful women as possible." Or, "I want to satisfy my urge to kiss or have sex with someone." "I want to have a boyfriend or girlfriend because all my friends have somebody and I do not want to be alone." Dating is filled with plenty of selfishness.

Courting is taking the time to learn about a person with the intention to make a commitment. Discussing purpose and future dreams and aspirations helps determine future planning and possible teamwork if you are considering marriage. When courting, we are able to look and see the person in a different light. If you have been dating with little or no success in relationships, perhaps a new picture (courting) may help.

Courting is often **not** considered when a unmarried person is being driven by lust. Dating is usually connected with lust.

Lust is a desire to benefit self at the expense of others. If my mind is to benefit me, I am not interested in how my date treats or responds to other people. I am not concerned about another's interests. I am concerned about me. Through movies, music, books and video, singles in our society are continually being presented with an idea that there really is something to love at first sight. It presents the idea that love is about us and what we get instead of it being about others and laying down our lives. Sacrifice. Although some have had success with the concept of love at first sight. This is the exception, not the norm.

Here is where the rubber meets the road. There are many definitions for the word love. If a person wants to have a true love relationship and be happy, they must accept God's definition of love. God's definition is best.

Remember, I shared earlier a person's definition will determine their destination? God is Love! He actually shows what love looks like. Everyone, who has been deeply hurt in relationships, will eventually have to look at the fact they may have ignored what true love looked like because we looked past God. If we accept His demonstration and definition we will not be tricked. If the definition of love I am sharing with you were a mathematical equation it would be GOD=Love. They are one and the same, not two different things. This is where many have been deceived.

Jesus also taught us how to love while He was on the earth, so we have to examine if we are really loving or lusting. Love gives. God so loved the world that He gave...His Son. He gave His best to those who did not deserve it. To have a great relationship, this principle must be learned and practiced. It is a principle of the kingdom.

In dating, many are looking to get from the relationship. As an unmarried person, who may be contemplating marriage, you should want to make sure you are a faithful person and find someone who will be faithful. Faithfulness is discovered during courting.

Just a suggestion, throw dating out the window, courting is the way to go!

I am going to make another bold statement. Many times, though not at all times, what people call love at first sight is really lust. I think it is imperative to know the difference between love and lust. I better define love and lust. We may refer to this definition again later. I got this definition from a great author and teacher of men, the late Edwin Cole. It has served me well in helping others in relationships.

He defined love as **the desire to benefit another at the expense of self.** Lust then, **is the desire to benefit self at the expense of another.** I will use these definitions throughout this resource. I believe, if you grasp them, they will help you immensely.

Most individuals who do not take the time to consider the difference between dating and courting end up in relationships that become adulterous (unfaithful). Our creator expects us to be faithful if we become a marriage partner to another and our marriage partner to be faithful to us.

God is love and God is Faithful. Faithfulness is a dimension of love. Do not get married without this trait being strong. Faithfulness is best developed during times of adversity. Friends tend to have the qualities consistent with God's love and we often overlook them as possible life covenant partners.

Faithfulness inspires trust. Trust is absolutely needed to have a strong relationship of celebration, not toleration.

May I say it again marriage is serious!

> Marriage is honorable in all, and the bed undefiled: but whoremongers and adulterers God will judge. **Hebrews 13:4**

Here a very potent verse of scripture which must be viewed in light of the kingdom of God message.

- *Chapter Four* -

MARRIAGE IS HONORABLE

Marriage speaks of covenant. God is a covenant maker and keeper. If we are growing into the image of Christ, and I define image as an exact likeness, we must be people of covenant.

The classifications of whoremonger and adulterers speak of people who were not keepers of covenant. In fact, adulterers are covenant breakers. The demonstration of covenant breaking is what has created the fear in many to get committed in covenant.

There are a lot of unmarried individuals just terrified of the idea of getting married. They have seen many bad experiences of marriage ending in divorce. Some having lived in homes where there was so much bickering and fighting between parents, they have made vows never to get married. These are known as spoken curses.

Others have witnessed the pain of relationships destroyed by unfaithfulness. This does not have to be you! There may be some bad models, but there are many doing marriage right. Be encouraged and don't be afraid. Be bold, be strong for the Lord your God is with you!

Let me take time to make a bold statement: Marriage to the right individual can be the BOMB! Excuse me. I come from a Pentecostal background and sometimes speak in other tongues (languages we were not normally born with). Let me interpret those tongues: *it can be very wonderful!*

In order to see the intent of the Lord, in marriage, we need to look at the origin of marriage. Let's go to the beginning. **Genesis 2:18-25**

> And the LORD God said, "It is not good that man should be alone; I will make him a helper comparable to him." Out of the ground the LORD God formed every beast of the field and every bird of the air, and brought them to Adam to see what he would call them. And whatever Adam called each living creature, that *was* its name. So Adam gave names to all cattle, to the birds of the air, and to every beast of the field. But for Adam there was not found a helper comparable to him.
>
> And the LORD God caused a deep sleep to fall on Adam, and he slept; and He took one of his ribs, and closed up the flesh in its place.
> Then the rib which the LORD God had taken from man He made into a woman, and He brought her to the man.
>
> And Adam said:
> "This *is* now bone of my bones

And flesh of my flesh;
She shall be called Woman,
Because she was taken out of Man."

Therefore a man shall leave his father and mother and be joined to his wife, and they shall become one flesh.

And they were both naked, the man and his wife, and were not ashamed.

Adam, the word of God says, "Was alone and it was **not** good!"

Everything the Lord God had made to this point was good. Yet He states, Adam's state of being alone was not good. With all of the animals of creation surrounding him, the beauty of all the earth, this condition of being isolated, detached and solitary concerned the Father. So, He created Eve. Eve was called his wife. Though they were two people, they were to be one in purpose.

A marriage in which two people fully understand God created mankind with a specific purpose, and they are committed to be people with the same purpose helping each other to achieve His purpose, they will have a very happy marriage.

What was the purpose given to Adam by the Lord in which he needed a helper comparable to himself? Let's see what the word of God says:

So God created man in His *own* image; in the image of God He created him; male and female He created them. Then God blessed them, and

God said to them, "Be fruitful and multiply; fill the earth and subdue it; have dominion over the fish of the sea, over the birds of the air, and over every living thing that moves on the earth." **Genesis 1:27-28**

I want to suggest the purpose of this couple was to steward the earth by sharing responsibility for managing on behalf of the Creator in His image and His likeness. They were together to release the keys of friendship, fellowship and discipleship. **They were to release the kingdom of God in the earth.** This was their purpose.

One great challenge in our society is that many people are getting married and not understanding God's purpose for marriage. The Holy Scriptures declare in the gospel of Matthew 6:33, "seek first the Kingdom of God and His righteousness and all these things shall be added unto you."

If God's intent is that we seek the kingdom, could it be the purpose of marriage was to demonstrate the kingdom of God in the earth by covenant? I would like to suggest this as a strong possibility.

Jehovah God enjoyed friendship (covenant) with Adam and Eve. He enjoyed fellowship (intimacy) with them. And His last command was to be fruitful and multiply. Many have thought this had to do with making babies, but I suspect it had to do with training (making disciples) of those who were born in the ways of the Creator.

- **If the revelation of the kingdom of God is**

received by those contemplating marriage and planned to be practiced, they will have a marriage made in heaven. This is working from the heavenly blueprint made manifest in the earth.

I want to clearly state again, there is nothing wrong with the institution of marriage. You just want to follow the guidelines I believe are clearly set forth in the scriptures to help make a wise choice. Marriage is honorable and need not to be feared. It can and will bring great blessing into your life when engaged soberly.

For men, the word of God promises blessing for both the man and his spouse. He who finds a wife, finds a good thing and obtains favor of the Lord. A life long friend and the favor of God.

What an honorable blessing!

Chapter Five

MARRIAGE IS A HIGH CALLING

For Zion's sake I will not hold My peace, and for
Jerusalem's sake I will not rest,
Until her righteousness goes forth as brightness,
And her salvation as a lamp *that* burns.
The Gentiles shall see your righteousness,
And all kings your glory.
You shall be called by a new name,
Which the mouth of the LORD will name.
You shall also be a crown of glory
In the hand of the LORD,
And a royal diadem
In the hand of your God.
You shall no longer be termed Forsaken,
Nor shall your land any more be termed Desolate;
But you shall be called Hephzibah,
and your land Beulah;
For the LORD delights in you,
And your land shall be married.
For *as* a young man marries a virgin,
So shall your sons marry you;
And *as* the bridegroom rejoices over the bride,
So shall your God rejoice over you.
Isaiah 62:1-5

Newlyweds bring a variety of expectations to marriage. But what are God's expectations for the marriage relationship? He designed the institution. What did He have in mind when established it? As an unmarried man, it is important to know the Father's heart on how a man is to treat a wife.

One window on God's perspective comes from His own "marriage" to Israel. The prophet Isaiah portrays the relationship between the Lord and His people as a marriage.

Let us look and notice what God as the bridegroom does for His bride.

- He protects and purifies her

- He honors and values her

- He identifies Himself with her, as signified by giving her new names.

Centuries later, Paul echoed Isaiah's bridal portrait of God and Israel when he described the marriage between Christ and the church. Once again, the bridegroom shows His love by protecting and purifying His bride, honoring and valuing her and identifying himself with her. Paul exhorted Christians to build their marriages on a similar basis.

We must ask the question, is this the way we view marriage?

If you are contemplating marriage, consider if you and your partner see marriage as a high calling and as your responsibility to serve each other in the ways described.

This is the heart of a biblical foundation for marriage.

There can be no greater love commitment expressed between two people, than to exhibit the character God has shown Israel and Christ has shown towards the church.

Before you say I do, it is important for you, if you are an unmarried single man, to understand what God expects of a man taking on a bride.

We are created in His image and His likeness to represent Him in the earth. Just as He purified and protected Israel, He wants us to do the same for our covenant partner.

- To protect: to cover or shield from something that would destroy or injure...guard, defend.

- To purify: to make free from anything that might injure or lower the quality. Not mixed with anything else.

- To honor: public admiration, outward respect and high moral standards of behavior.

- To value: to think highly of, to estimate the worth of.

- Give her a good name and identify with her. This is a great challenge but with the help of the Holy Spirit this can be accomplished.

For unmarried men contemplating making a life's

commitment to another person to build a life together, it is important to know these attributes are necessary to walk in the high calling of God...friendship...oops marriage.

I continue to be inspired to provoke you to think of how important friendship is in the process of having a fruitful marriage.

You are becoming a person of covenant. Flee the mentality to not be committed to others and learn to be a covenant keeper. Courting is the way to protect yourself and defeat the spirit of Jezebel's seductive lure to non-committed relationships.

- Chapter Six -

THE SPIRIT OF DESPERATION

And in that day seven women shall take hold of one man, saying, "We will eat our own food and wear our own apparel; Only let us be called by your name, To take away our reproach." **Isaiah 4:1**

I knew I could not get through this whole book without dealing with some spiritual warfare (deliverance). Well on second thought, this whole resource is an exercise in warfare. Fighting to empower the unmarried is an exercise in changing mentalities. In this chapter, I want to uncover a spirit which seeks to destroy females in their relationships. The spirit of desperation.

In relationships there will be warfare to maintain relationships which will be godly. I will share some thoughts to provoke some honest searching among unmarried women. There is no easy way to explore this, except to hit it head on.

It is not my intent to declare there are no men who are desperate. In fact, let me say it plainly, there are many men who are desperate to have a wife and do not.

In this chapter, I aim to speak as a father of spiritual daughters. I want to speak to daughters because this spirit (attitude) is destroying women in far greater numbers than men.

The spirit of God thought enough of it to have it dealt with by the prophet Isaiah. The feeling provoked by Isaiah 4:1 is prevalent today. It seems like desperation. The causes for this behavior can be found in some ladies today and may be at work to keep them from healthy relationships with the opposite sex.

Truth empowers a person to walk in freedom and liberty. I offer this text in the hopes it will provoke inward evaluations of pride, vanity, anger and those attitudes which work against being "found" by your Boaz.

There seems to be a feeling among some females there are not enough men to go around. To that statement some of you, who are ladies, probably said, Amen!

However, giving in to that line of thinking can produce internal deception opening the door to desperation. If women keep repeating that particular falsehood, they may convince themselves there are no good men around. Can we be real?

Many women never get away from their neighborhood, place of work or their state in order to have interacted with enough men to make such a statement. If you consider that many individuals limit themselves to courting within their own culture, it becomes difficult to understand how this statement is perpetuated. But it is.

I submit it is not true. There are many good and available men. But you may not know where to find them! Don't allow the lie to exist in your head.

In our society, some ladies have made a point of getting involved in (unhealthy) illegal relationships in order to have a mate because they are desperate. Many would never admit this.

There are women making choices to settle for less than the best they can have by lowering themselves and dating married men. Others have been involved sexual relationships outside the bonds of marriage for the sake of meeting material needs. Many types of behaviors motivated by a feeling of desperation often lead to great pain and disillusionment, in some instances even death.

I have known many females who had 'friends'. Men who came by to do some needed task who they ended up sleeping with them as payment. Some ladies used men to gain finances and ended up having children outside of wedlock and creating situations of difficulty for all parties involved because their was no real love or commitment involved.

Some get involved in relationships with incarcerated men for sexual relations. Some marry, many times before their intended has an opportunity to prove there has been a change in the thinking which produced the bondage of incarceration. When the spirit of desperation is at work destruction and foolishness is not far behind.

Desperation has us do things we never would if there was no pressure. The spirit of desperation must be defeated!

While growing up during the late 60's or early 70's there was a popular song in that day by a singing group called the Isley Brothers with lyrics saying, "If you can't be with the one you love, honey, love the one you're with." This type of thinking has to be rejected by unmarried women wanting to please their Lord and have a relationship which will be fulfilling.

There was a popular song which I called the anthem of desperation, "Saving All My Love for You," by Whitney Houston, which was sung about someone else's man. This song represents the attitude of the selfish. Not those who are sold out to God. It produce in many, a justification for being with someone already married.

- **Choices made out of desperation will never amount to anything good. God, by His Spirit, leads and guides us. He does not put pressure on us to make decisions.**

This particular passage of scripture in Isaiah 4:1 is a continuation of thought Isaiah begins in chapter three. I must include this chapter in the book to show there may be a correlation between the women encountering this type of thinking during Isaiah's day and unmarried women in society who become overcome by this type of thinking in our day and time.

Isaiah begin to lay out God's message to His people of their missing the mark with Him. Israel has turned away from obeying the teachings of God. Because God is righteous and just, He pronounces His opinion and decision.

When desperation comes to women, pressure to do anything to have a man, it may be an indication there has been a moving away from obeying the scriptures.

Part of God's justice dealt with the daughter's of Jerusalem and their "independent" of God attitudes: Isaiah 3:16

Moreover the LORD says:
"Because the daughters of Zion are haughty,
And walk with outstretched necks
And wanton eyes,
Walking and mincing *as* they go,
Making a jingling with their feet,
Therefore the Lord will strike with a scab
The crown of the head of the daughters of Zion,
And the LORD will uncover their secret parts."
In that day the Lord will take away the finery:
The jingling anklets, the scarves, and the crescents;
The pendants, the bracelets, and the veils;
The headdresses, the leg ornaments, and the
    headbands;
The perfume boxes, the charms,
    and the rings;
The nose jewels,
    the festal apparel, and the mantles;
The outer garments, the purses, and the mirrors;
The fine linen, the turbans, and the robes.

And so it shall be:
Instead of a sweet smell there will be a stench;
Instead of a sash, a rope;
Instead of well-set hair, baldness;
Instead of a rich robe, a girding of sackcloth;
And branding instead of beauty.
Your men shall fall by the sword,
And your mighty in the war.
Her gates shall lament and mourn,
And she *being* desolate shall sit on the ground.
Isaiah 3:16-26

As I read the pages of Isaiah, I can see a spirit at work producing a woman who is proud and feels like, "I don't need a man," then being brought to a place of depression and desperation.

The women of the day saying I will get my own food and clothing, only marry me to remove my reproach.

While things are well for them, they are using their beauty flirting with men, using men and never feeling the need to be in a committed relationship. They value their beauty, jewelry, and sweet smell. They are full of vanity.

I want to caution every daughter of the Lord against the spirit of pride, which opens the door to the spirit of desperation. It is a spirit (attitude) which works with vanity.

The Lord God of Israel judged the proud look of the women of that day with baldness, unpleasant smells (perhaps bad female discharges), loss of jewelry (which could speak of finances, prosperity) and loss of beauty. A spirit of shame would be their portion. Consider this verse in the book of Proverbs:

> When *pride* comes, then comes *shame*; But with the humble *is* wisdom. **Proverbs 11:2**

It seems women had come to such a state in their personal outward appearance and attitude no one wanted to be bothered with marrying them. This produced what I have termed the "spirit of desperation."

> And in that day seven women shall take hold of one man, saying, "We will eat our own food and wear our own apparel; Only let us be called by your name, To take away our reproach." **Isaiah 4:1**

Let's bring this into our generation. We live in the age of the liberated woman. Sometimes it seems she's so liberated she is free from even God!

She seemingly is willing to do almost anything to have a man. Before you say I Do, please be sure the decision to be married is not fueled by the spirit of desperation.

Moreover the LORD says:
"Because the daughters of Zion are haughty,
And walk with outstretched necks
And wanton eyes,
Walking and mincing *as* they go,
Making a jingling with their feet,
Therefore the Lord will strike with a scab
The crown of the head of the daughters

of Zion,
And the LORD will uncover their secret parts."
Isaiah 3:16-17

As a daughter of the Lord, before you say I do,
examine yourself or have someone with whom you
are able to discuss if these character traits are present
in your life on a consistent basis.

The following are things which can open the door to
functioning from a place of desperation:

- Haughtiness

- Wanton eyes

- Flirtatious walking

- Wearing jewelry that attracts attention to certain
  parts of the body seductively.

Do you know anyone, who as a daughter of God is
"keeping" some man who is not working or has a
place of his own? Or, do you know someone dating a
man who is married, promising them he is going to
get a divorce, but never getting out of the relationship?
Involved in a relationship where there is physical
abuse, just because they don't want to be lonely?

All these are signs of a desperate person. It is time to
be free from the spirit of desperation!

Lose yourself from thinking inspired by soul ties with
friends, who have these type of relationships. They
are not healthy and you deserve better.

Pride created the problem in Israel and so the answer

then must be humility. Proud women drive men away.

May I offer a fresh thought? Men want to be prince charming. Naturally speaking, men want to rescue the damsel in distress. They want to be prince charming. Are you killing your own giants in front of potential suitors?

If men are made to feel there is no need for them, why would they commit to a life of not being needed. There are a lot of young ladies who kill their own dragon's and slay their own giants and thus drive away potential suitors.

You can be so independent, you release an attitude (spirit) of the un-covenanted one (Jezebel) the spirit of independence and keep potential Boaz's from approaching.

God never intended for you as a virgin or unmarried person to have to settle for a relationship out of desperation. This is an age of desperation. There is only one remedy for protection against the spirit of desperation. A lifestyle of humility.

Humility produces and provides:

- Honor and riches

- Revival

- Exaltation

- Grace

Humility is a chief characteristic of the life and nature of Christ.

The word of God shows how, through humbling Himself, Christ was raised to a place of exaltation over the forces of darkness. Desperation functions out of darkness. Listen to the scriptures:

> Let this mind be in you, which was also in Christ Jesus: Who, being in the form of God, thought it not robbery to be equal with God: But made himself of no reputation, and took upon him the form of a servant, and was made in the likeness of men: And being found in fashion as a man, he humbled himself, and became obedient unto death, even the death of the cross. Wherefore God also hath highly exalted him, and given him a name which is above every name: That at the name of Jesus every knee should bow, of things in heaven, and things in earth, and things under the earth; And that every tongue should confess that Jesus Christ is Lord, to the glory of God the Father. **Philippians 2:5-10**

This same kingdom principle will work for any woman who desires to be free from the spirit of desperation.

Prayer:
Dear Father, I thank you for my sisters who love you and who you love. I take authority over the spirits assigned to stir up desperation in the lives of your daughters.

You declare in your word, whatever we bind or forbid on earth will be bound of forbidden in the heaven and whatever we loose or permit in the earth will be loosed or permitted in heaven. I bind the power of Leviathan (pride) in the life of my sisters. I command spirits of desperation, vanity, haughtiness and lust to leave in the power of the name of Christ and loose within them the spirits of humility, honor, grace, meekness and love.

I declare the spirit of Jezebel, the spirit which does not want to commit to covenant to be broken in their lives. I declare my sisters to be vessels of honor, covenant keepers, not desperate but whole.

I pray and break all ungodly soul ties with any person or persons who foster lies in their lives rooted in pride. Satan was proud and a liar and they are committed to be in covenant with Christ and the truth. They know the truth and the truth makes them free. Today, they are free from the spirit of desperation, embarrassment, reproach and any other spirit (attitude or thought life) which is not consistent with the word of God and a godly life.

They are daughters of God and are blessed.

These things do not bring reproach. They represent the blessing of the Lord. May the spirit of desperation be far from all who read the exhortation of these pages. May you be blessed as a daughter of the Lord forever more.

Chapter Seven

IN TO ME SEE
(INTIMACY)

And they were both naked, the man and his wife, and were not ashamed. **Genesis 2:25**

This chapter in Genesis closes with this verse. Locked within these words is a powerful truth. The man and his wife had no secrets. This picture is one of transparency of heart and relationship. The man and his wife, as well as, man and his God enjoyed wonderful covenant intimacy which was demonstrated by no shame. When there is transparent communication, there can be intimacy. With honesty there is no shame.

After the fall of Adam which was brought about by Adam's pride and disobedience, the picture is now sharply contrasted.

And they heard the voice of the LORD God walking in the garden in the cool of the day: and Adam and his wife hid themselves from the presence of the LORD God amongst the trees of the garden.

And the LORD God called unto Adam, and

said unto him, Where art thou?
And he said, I heard thy voice in the garden,
and I was afraid, because I was naked; and I
hid myself. **Genesis 3:8-10**

When there is no honest communication, or a heart
having to hide or be deceitful, there is only fear and
covering up. This hinders in-to-me-see (intimacy).

Before you say I do, every unmarried person should
consider their ability to communicate their feelings to
their intended. In counseling couples who were
having trouble in their marriages, one thing has
become very clear to me. When there is no
communication, there is no intimacy.

When there is no intimacy there will usually be
trouble. I did not say sex, I said intimacy. Intimacy
comes by talking.

When I was a young man growing up, I was attracted
to a young lady and wanted her phone number. I
wanted to know her. As we talked on the phone, I was
able to get to know her likes and dislikes. I was able
to learn about her dreams, goals, fears and what
things we may have had in common. I was able to **see
into her.** She was spiritually naked.

Likewise, I uncovered myself and shared my likes,
favorite things, fears, goals and dreams. She was able
to **see into me.** We were communicating, open and
honest.

When two people become spiritually naked through
words, intimacy can happen. Intimacy is spiritual

before it ever becomes physical.

Jesus identifies words are spiritual when He said in John 6:63, "The words I speak are spirit and they are life."

Because we are spiritual beings, our words are spirit. We can make heart (spiritual) connections. This is necessary if you are going to choose to marry someone. (Just a side note: this is the reason I suggest young people not spend too much time on the phone with each other and there is no thought of marriage. It can only lead to nakedness in the natural, if you know what I mean!)

Let's look at a biblical picture. In the book of Genesis, Adam had a covenant relationship with God. He shared in-to-me-see. His life was transparent before God. Nothing was hidden. He walked with God and talked with God. Adam knew God and God knew Adam. After the fall of Adam and Eve into sin, he became fearful and wanted to hide himself.

These things he did in the natural, but it shadowed a strong spiritual principal. Intimacy is about nakedness or transparency.

In order for there to be a strong covenant of faithfulness there has to be transparency, in-to-me-see...see into me. If I am contemplating marriage, the ability to be transparent is a must. It is a foundational key to faithfulness.

Before you say I do, as an unmarried person, you have an opportunity to develop intimacy, IN TO ME SEE with our Lord. We are actually married / joined (in covenant) to Christ.

What, as an unmarried person, should you look for in the person you want to marry? Here are some suggestions.

You want a person who can be intimate and you want to be a person who can be intimate. My response can be summed up into a few biblical actions which show intimacy with God.

If one cannot be consistently intimate (open, honest and transparent) with God, it will be difficult to be intimate with others.

How do I develop the kind of intimacy (transparency) necessary to have a healthy fruitful relationship with another person? I believe we must develop and master at least these five things:

1. Praise

2. Worship

3. Giving

4. Prayer

5. Repentance

If we are able to consistently do these five things with God, we will be able to communicate well with an intended spouse.

- **I want to emphatically declare, if the person you are thinking of entering into the covenant of**

marriage with has not learned to do these things towards God, it will be hard for the individual to give them to you. These are necessary ingredients of communication for intimacy.

When most relationships are in trouble it is usually stated there is a lack of communication. I would like to suggest to you several attributes necessary for good communication.

Praise: A person who can thank God for the things He does, has done or will do will be able to say thank you and appreciate you for what you do.

Worship: If a person is not able to take the time to honor God for who He is, honoring Him for His character, he will never be able to appreciate or honor you for who you are as a person.

Giving: If a person is not able to open their heart to be able to give, of time, money and using their gifts for God's service to Him chances are they will be selfish towards you.

Prayer: If a person is not able to open up to God and cast their cares on Him, they may not be able to open up and share their feelings with you.

Repentance: If a person has not come to the place where he or she can admit they have missed the mark with God and be sorry and be willing to change for Him, chances are they will not be will to do this with you.

For a believer, when we confess our sins and ask

forgiveness of God for them, we enter into covenant with God. I want to give a definition of covenant. A covenant is an agreement, a promise between two parties to be committed to their relationship. A covenant is only as strong as the trustworthiness of the parties involved. Transparency in communication is of the utmost importance to show trustworthiness.

It is important we see ourselves as married to Christ. If our marriage covenant is healthy with God, we will have a good head start to have healthy covenant relationships with others.

I think you should consider each of these very significant areas and measure first your level of competence in them. If you pass the test, then you should evaluate the level of the person you are going to share life with. These are necessary tools for healthy communication and friendship.

Almost every relationship joined in marriage enters into trouble when there is no communication.

Before you say I Do, may I suggest to practice communicating and developing in-to-me-see with and on God!

Chapter Eight

IS IT LOVE OR LUST?

Beloved, let us love one another: for love is of God; and every one that loveth is born of God, and knoweth God. He that loveth not knoweth not God; for **God is love.** 1 John 4:7-8

I believe, if there is one chapter in this resource I consider to be most important, this is the one. Before you say I Do, it is imperative to have a correct understanding of what love is. Better yet, WHO Love is.

This is usually the place where most relationships fall apart at the beginning.

I want to make another bold statement, **wrong definitions produce wrong thinking, which produce wrong conclusions, which produce wrong actions.**

If two people define the same words differently, they will come to different conclusions or judgments about the same thing. This then can become the seed bed for disharmony in a relationship.

This chapter is not the complete dictionary concerning love. It is just the small portion of revelation I have received.

I would like to share the glimpse of Christ I have received in this area. I want to provoke some new thoughts in you while you contemplate whether marriage is for you or if the timing is right.

Even though love is a four letter word, it is comprised of many characteristics. Each characteristic needs to be considered before making the ultimate decision of when to say I Do.

I have counseled many couples planning to get married. I have counseled those who have gotten married. I would ask them if they loved the person they were going to marry. They would respond, yes! I then would asked them to tell me why they loved the person they intended to marry.

The answers on the surface sounded wonderful to them, but many times revealed a lack of understanding of the true nature of love.

Many times a couple begins to answer: he has a good job, he has a nice car, he likes to take me out, buy me nice things and he is good looking. I like spending time with him. She can cook and takes care of a house. She is pretty and I love her. I like spending time with her. During these times of exchange, I often do not hear the essence of what love is or better yet, who Love is.

Let me, without shame, declare to you God is Love!

Many people act as if that two lettered word **is** isn't in the middle of God and Love. Without the word *is,* the idea is conveyed God and Love are two different things. The word is in the middle mean they are one and the same. With this in mind let us consider: God=Love.

> Beloved, let us love one another, for love is of God; and everyone who loves is born of God and knows God. He who does not love does not know God, **for God is love**. In this the love of God was manifested toward us, that God has sent His only begotten Son into the world, that we might live through Him. In this is love, not that we loved God, but that He loved us and sent His Son *to be* the propitiation for our sins. Beloved, if God so loved us, we also ought to love one another.
>
> No one has seen God at any time. If we love one another, God abides in us, and His love has been perfected in us. By this we know that we abide in Him, and He in us, because He has given us of His Spirit. And we have seen and testify that the Father has sent the Son *as* Savior of the world. Whoever confesses that Jesus is the Son of God, God abides in him, and he in God. And we have known and believed the love that God has for us. **God is love**, and he who abides in love abides in God, and God in him. **1 John 4:7-16**

The Scriptures also make another point that has to be examined:

Behold what manner of love the Father has bestowed on us, that we should be called children of God! Therefore the world does not know us, because it did not know Him. Beloved, now we are children of God; and it has not yet been revealed what we shall be, but we know that when He is revealed, we shall be like Him, for we shall see Him as He is. **1 John 3:1-3**

If the two people who are contemplating getting married are not clear about the nature of the Creator, it is going to be a much more difficult relationship than it has to be.

The human tendency of people without an understanding of their Creator is towards selfishness. This is the nature of all humans and is the root of imperfection and missing the mark in life (better known as sin).

God is Love. The deep rooted spiritual truth in this statement is God is selfless. This can be seen in a practical way. The bible states in John 3:16 a powerful truth, For God so loved the world that He gave His only begotten Son. The nature of God is He is a giver first and foremost. And when He gives, He gives His best. The love of God, is also willing to sacrifice its best for others who are not in the position to return it. This is what builds strong relationships.

A look at 1 John 3:16 seems to parallel this same point:

By this we know love, because He laid down

His life for us. And we also ought to lay down *our* lives for the brethren. **1 John 3:16**

The reason we must begin at this starting point is because everything needing to be learned about love is locked in the nature of the Creator.

Let me share with you how I discovered this revelation of Love.

Earlier I spoke of missing the mark. I was in a worship service and the teacher, Bishop Larry Jackson, was ministering on the subject of the glory of God. He read a familiar passage from the bible Romans 3:23 which says, For all have sinned and come short of the glory of God.

The Greek word for sin is **harmartia** which means to miss the mark in a moral sense concerning God's laws in word or deed. When we choose not to follow God's moral standard, we choose our own standard and it becomes a choice for what benefits us. This is more commonly called selfishness. All sin is rooted in choices made to benefit ourselves at the expense of others or God's desire.

Bishop Jackson then led us to a passage in the word of God in the Old Testament in the book of Exodus 33 where Moses asks to see what Paul declared we lacked, the glory of God.

Moses requested to see the glory of God and God said He could. Look at these verses:

Now the Lord descended in the cloud and

stood with him there, and proclaimed the name of the Lord. And the Lord passed before him and proclaimed, "The Lord, the Lord God, merciful and gracious, longsuffering, and abounding in goodness and truth, keeping mercy for thousands, forgiving iniquity and transgression and sin, by no means clearing the guilty, visiting the iniquity of the fathers upon the children and the children's children to the third and the fourth generation."

So Moses made haste and bowed his head toward the earth, and worshiped. **Exodus 34:5-8**

The glory of God is the full weight of His nature, all that makes God, Love! Every human has a void or place within himself or herself looking for God (Love).

When God reveals Himself to Moses, he sees complete mercy, grace, long-suffering, abundant goodness, truth, forgiveness and justice. The very sight of Love (God's glory) caused Moses to bow down and worship.

When we think of what we need in a relationship, we must keep in mind we are imperfect beings who will need only what God can offer.

We say we need love, but let's interpret what we mean literally. If we are imperfect, we will need someone who will show mercy when we need mercy. We will need someone who will forgive us when we need forgiveness. We will want someone who will be kind to us or gracious to us. We will need a mate who will be able to at times put up with us be patient (long suffering). A relationship will not last if there is no truth. All of us desire to be treated justly. What we are looking for is God.

It is what we to come short of, it is the nature of God.

As I pondered what Moses asked for, I began to see tangible evidence of things to look for during the courtship period which will help in the evaluation process of a covenant partner.

> Be ye not unequally yoked together with unbelievers: for what fellowship hath righteousness with unrighteousness? and what communion hath light with darkness? And what concord hath Christ with Belial? or what part hath he that believeth with an infidel? **2 Corinthians 6:14-15**

Love is comprised of many attributes added together to make the whole. You must look for equal parts of the whole during courting, which will take time. Truth, forgiveness, mercy, compassion, justice, grace, faithfulness, holiness and long suffering are attributes of Christ. If we watch throughout the scriptures, we see Him demonstrate all these characteristics.

We are not fooled when we see them in print, we should not settle for less when choosing a life's partner in the natural. These traits are tangible. They also have one consistent dimension consistent with a loving heart, sacrifice or laying down one's life.

A willingness to lay down our right in order for us to walk in harmony. When we forgive, suffer long, show mercy, and speak truth, we die to selfishness and come alive to selflessness. All the attributes of a faithful person are developed through being yielded to others in authority over us. It takes humility.

Love is about dying to our selfish desires!

I have a new saying, before you get married you don't need just a marriage license, you need a spiritual death certificate and a toe tag!

You may be saying to yourself a toe tag.

Yes, a toe tag! At the morgue when you have a dead body the way the mortician is able to identify the deceased is by their toe tag.

Dead people don't lie. Dead people don't cheat. Dead people do not curse you out. Dead people don't control you. Dead people don't beat you. Don't hate your family. I think you get my meaning. Also for the believer, death is the only way to the resurrected life. Don't forget the toe tag!

Love is the very thing everyone is looking for. The truth is God in us is who everyone is looking for, in each other. Let me further explain my perspective on love as borne out of the reality of the scriptures.

Love is not just a feeling. Love is action. Love is what is done. There is only one real definition which matters:

God is Love.

If you are contemplating getting married and you are a believer in the Lord Jesus Christ, you should not be dating or courting anyone who does not have a relationship with God and His word. The only thing that person can be consistently is **selfish. All that is connected with God and the Holy Spirit produces selflessness.**

The flesh and demons inspire self centeredness and selfishness.

You have to admit to yourself, if you are dating someone not a person of faith, you are having challenges with the person being concerned about themselves and their friends more than you.

This might be difficult but you may need to get beyond this person. It is not time to say I do! It is not even the time to say "I might." Get out of the relationship. I have told the daughters and sons of the house, do it NOW!

Their response to this suggestion is, "I don't want to hurt their feelings." My response is, "Jesus is a healer and He will take care of them and their feelings!"

Your purpose and destiny to become Christ like could be in jeopardy. Before you say I Do, you must be able to pass the definition of love test. I will give you the answer so you can pass the test: Shhhhhhh! Listen close. **GOD IS LOVE!** You need someone with a real relationship with God. Don't settle for less.

- *Chapter Nine* -
GOD'S PORTRAIT
OF A HUSBAND

For your Maker *is* your husband, The LORD
of hosts *is* His name; And your Redeemer *is*
the Holy One of Israel; He is called the God
of the whole earth. **Isaiah 54:5**

From the words of Holy Scripture, comes help from
above to give prophetic vision into what it takes to be
a good husband. The function of husband is one
undertaken by many men without a clearly defined
picture to help successfully navigate very serious
waters.

It is my hope that this chapter will give an unmarried
man, who is interested in being a good husband, a
clear "game plan" to fully communicate the love he
has for his bride. I also hope it will provide unmarried
women things to consider if contemplating marriage.

You should know what your maker considers a good
husband. I believe, if you do not violate the principles
of scripture stated you will be blessed. These are not
my words, they are the words of scripture.

Perhaps the prophet Isaiah's description of God, the "husband" of Israel (Isaiah 54:5) can help. There can be no greater model or example of a godly husband than God Himself.

I would like to suggest some of the points set forth in the verses found in Isaiah 54 describing a godly husband:

- **A good husband helps his wife find fulfillment.** In verses 1-3. The Lord speaks prophetically and with confidence of a better future. Enlarge your tents, lengthen your cords, you shall expand and grow. He gives positive reinforcement.

- **A good husband seeks to allay her fears.** Verses 4,14 and 15 clearly speak to helping a wife overcome any fears she may have. This is what may be needed to provide a sense of security.

- **A good husband builds up his wife's reputation.** He seeks to be aware of not doing things to cause shame, disgrace or reproach. Verse 4.

- **A good husband displays godly character**: being mindful of the attributes of God's faithfulness... Loyalty, devotion, truth, commitment, dedication etc.

- **A good husband does not allow prolonged conflict or lingering anger to keep him separated from his wife.** (Verses 6-8) The scripture says, "for a mere moment I have forsaken you, but with great mercies I will gather you. I hid my face for a moment, but with everlasting kindness I will have mercy on you." It speaks of momentary separation but a right attitude and spirit of reconciliation.

- **A good husband replaces anger with kindness.** (verse 8) see above.

- **A good husband brings comfort to her in the midst of stress** (verses 11-12). Notice in these verses the way the language of scripture seems to communicate the use of jewels to bring comfort. Colorful gems, sapphires, rubies, crystals and precious stones! Brothers we cannot go wrong with the jewels!

- **A good husband will instruct the children in spiritual matters** (verse 13) and all thy children shall be taught of the Lord...the responsibility of children knowing the Lord should not be thought of as a function of the wife/mother alone.

- **A good husband will protect his wife from danger and threats** (verses 16-17) A good husband is one who will see to it no weapon natural or verbal formed against his spouse will prosper. A life of prayer is a must!

God's relationship with Israel is a picture of God's committed love. I believe it would be wisdom for any man before getting married to see where he would measure up on God's scale of being a good husband.

Please consider these principles to see if they will help being a better husband or a great husband. What a gift to give the woman who would be your wife!

If you are married and reading this work, perhaps you too could benefit from these principles. God gives us a good snapshot of what being a good husband is all about.

Prayer:
Lord, you have created me for your pleasure and I
desire to be a good husband. You have shown in your
teachings what a good husband looks like. You are a
great 'Husband' to your people.

Please help me to apply these principles. I want my
marriage to reflect you and your love. I want to be a
fountain of blessing to my wife. May the kingdom
been seen in my covenant relationship.

- Chapter Ten -

GOD'S PORTRAIT
OF A WIFE

Who can find a virtuous wife? For her worth
is far above rubies. **Proverbs 31:10**

Proverbs 31 is one of the most well loved passages in
the word of God. If practiced it will produce one
powerful woman in the Lord. Any woman considering
entering into the covenant of marriage would do well
to consider how she measures up to God's standard of
a good wife.

Before you say I do, you want to be a wise woman.
Proverbs 31 is describing a woman of wisdom and the
corresponding actions that declare her wise.

In the bible wisdom is personified as a woman. In
fact, it also says wisdom is more valuable than any
riches. In an earlier chapter we learned, God is love.

In this chapter, we learn God is wise. My endeavor is
to provoke you to not make a decision to get married
without God in the core of the relationship. These are
practical, tangible ways of manifesting God in the
relationship. If you are an unmarried man you want

to make sure you are familiar with characteristics identified in this chapter in evaluating a virtuous wife.

It will serve to help you find the wife of your dreams. She is a woman of God!

A good wife first and foremost fears the Lord! In verse 30 I don't think it could be said any better. Charm can be counterfeit and beauty will pass but a woman who fears the Lord shall be praised.

- **A good wife will do her husband good not evil all her days.** These words just practiced will release great blessing into a marriage relationship.

- **A good wife works hard and her diligence is rewarded.** Verses 13-16 and 21-22. Willing to work with her hands, provides food for her household, able to function in the marketplace.

- **A good wife not only looks after her own family, she is concerned about community.** Verse 20 She is not a self centered or selfish woman.

- **A good wife keeps herself attractive.** Verses 21-22. She is concerned about the appearance of herself and that of the family and it brings respect from others. She had purple, scarlet and fine linen which suggests fine things even if she had to make them.

- **A good wife causes her husband's reputation to grow** (building it up). Verse 23.

- **A good wife is a woman of strength & honor.** Verse 25. A good wife is not a door mat but a person who is secure and gracious not insecure and controlling. She is strong in the Lord and the power of His might.

- **<u>A good wife knows how to possess her tongue.</u>** Verses 26-27 She is a woman who releases wisdom, kind words, no gossiper. She also is not loud or stubborn.

- **<u>A good wife inspires praise from her family.</u>** This is the fruit and sign of a selfless life.

- **<u>A good wife has a meek and quiet spirit.</u>** 1 Peter 3:4

The word of God states this is precious in God's sight.

As a woman of God preparing herself for her future king, these words from God's word will help in becoming the wife God would desire you to be.

Prayer: Lord, thank you I am fearfully, wonderfully made and I desire to be a good wife to my husband. I am a woman of the kingdom and your principals defeat every principality set against my purpose. Please help me through the guidance of the Holy Spirit to become the kind of wife which shows your heart and releases your glory. I want to be a blessing to my husband and our marriage honor you.

- Chapter Eleven -

THE CONCLUSION OF THE WHOLE MATTER

Beloved, I wish above all things that thou mayest prosper and be in health, even as thy soul prospereth. For I rejoiced greatly, when the brethren came and testified of the truth that is in thee, even as thou walkest in the truth. I have no greater joy than to hear that my children walk in truth.
3 John 2-4

The Creator of the world desires our prospering in life. I have often taught in the church, you are born to be blessed not cursed. I feel a great mandate to encourage the unmarried to walk in truth. There is joy in walking in truth. God is a covenant making and keeping God.

In order to truly be blessed, we must abide by the covenant. The covenant is upheld by the truth and trust in God. We must do our part.

When it comes to relationships, it is important to know you have a purpose and destiny. Purpose can be destroyed, if we join ourselves to the wrong individuals. Many believers have become so skeptical of trusting others, they are living in the place called being noncommittal. This is a dangerous place considering benefitting one's self at the expense of another with no commitment is not Christ like. You must be person of truth.

I have simply tried to touch some areas of concern I see among the unmarried, in this season, as God restores the apostolic grace within the church. Many unmarried people are in local churches feeling like lepers and I believe it is time to see them healed and released from their bondage.

Good things can occur when there is dialog. I hope you will be encouraged to discuss some of the thoughts expressed in this resource.

I once again want to state, I do not consider myself to be right on all accounts shared. Through my studies, I want to stir dialog among youth groups, the unmarried, and church leaders to deal with what I believe is at the root of a lot of challenges in the church today.

If the unmarried are encouraged to find protection in Christ the covenant keeper and really explore the place of protection in the metaphor "a eunuch for the kingdom's sake'" even if you choose to get married, I believe you will have a prosperous soul and great joy and even spread great joy to many.

May grace and peace be multiplied to you.